Understanding Selective Mutism

A Beginner's Guide

LUCY NATHANSON

www.confidentchildren.co.uk

®

ISBN 978-1-78808-784-1
eISBN 978-1-78808-785-8

Cover design by Givi Phirtskhalava

To my friends and family who endlessly support me on my journey and passion for selective mutism.

To the children with selective mutism who have taught me so much and inspire me every day.

Contents

Introduction

Hello! Thank you for being here to increase your understanding of selective mutism. You may be a parent, family member, teacher, keyworker, therapist - whoever you are, you are here because you want to understand selective mutism more, to understand what these children are experiencing. There are many misconceptions surrounding this condition; I am thrilled to have the opportunity to provide content in a clear and concise way.

My name is Lucy Nathanson, I am a child therapist and founder of www.confidentchildren.co.uk. I have spent the last six years dedicating my life to helping children with selective mutism. Whilst on a school placement for my Applied Psychology and Sociology degree at university, I came across a child with selective mutism. The headteacher told me that the child had not spoken at all at school for two years. I was shocked. How was this possible? How could no one have helped this child in two years?! This was the first time I had heard of the condition; I didn't know of any official techniques, but I could see that what the school was doing was not working. School staff made comments such as: "He just won't talk", "We've tried everything", "Nothing works" – it was as though they had given up on the child. Given up on a five year old?!

I asked the headteacher if I could work with the child for the three weeks I was to be at the school. He agreed. I spent every afternoon with this boy and sure enough, little by little, he began to feel comfortable with me, began to make sounds and ultimately, he began to speak to me. By the end of my placement he was putting his hand up in class and answering questions. What I had done had worked and it was the best moment of my life.

At this stage, I was no specialist but somehow, I felt and knew what the child needed. It had been intuitive, but it had worked. I knew I wanted to help more and more children with selective mutism.

From there I began to learn specific techniques (a lot of which I had been doing intuitively without knowing they were 'techniques'). I took part in training with Maggie Johnson and Alison Wintgens (authors of *The Selective Mutism Resource Manual*). I travelled to New York, USA, completed training with the Child Mind Institute and took part in their Brave Buddies programme. I have also taken part in training at Kurtz Psychology Consulting PC and taken part in the WeSpeak programme. I have been a speaker at the SMIRA conference (selective mutism information and research association) in the UK twice, and have also spoken at the Languages and Emotions conference organised by the University of Silesia in Katowice, Poland, on two occasions. At the time of publication, my YouTube videos on selective mutism have exceeded 55,000 views.

The approach I follow is a combination of the approaches available, both in the UK and USA, and I adapt these to the specific child I'm working with.

As a result of working with schools and therapists internationally, I have found that there are often misconceptions of what selective mutism is. I have written this book to provide an introduction for people who would like to gain a greater understanding of selective mutism. Thank you for being here.

What Is Selective Mutism?

Selective Mutism (which I'll refer to as SM from now) is an anxiety disorder which can affect both children and adults. For the purposes of this book, I will be focusing on children with SM.

Children with SM can talk and are very confident doing so in situations where they feel comfortable. However, they are unable to talk in other situations.

To give you an example, a child may be able to talk at home, when they are with close family; however, they may become mute if a family friend is present. The child may not talk at school; their teacher may have never heard their voice, or perhaps they can talk to a few friends but not to others. Children often find it hard to talk in public situations such as at the park, in a restaurant, in the supermarket and so on. It is common that if a stranger asks the child a question, such as, "What is your name?" or "How old are you?", the child is unable to respond. They may freeze and cling onto their parent.

Some children with SM are unable to talk to their parent in public situations; other children can talk to their parent in front of others but are unable to respond directly to specific people or strangers.

It is not just strangers that children with SM may be unable to talk to; often there are familiar people in the child's life who they do not talk to; sometimes family members such as grandparents, uncles and aunts, family friends and so on.

Some children with SM find it equally difficult to talk to both adults and children. On the other hand, some children with SM are able to talk to children but not to adults, whereas others are able to talk to adults but find it difficult to talk to children.

As you can see, there is no 'typical' behaviour description – every single child is an individual and unique. I have never met two children who are exactly the same in their presentation of SM.

Please take a moment to reflect and apply the above to the child you know, to gain a deeper understanding of their unique SM – who they can and can't talk to and in what situations they are able or unable to talk.

Why Doesn't The Child Talk?

SM can be described as a phobia of speaking.

If you imagine a person who has a phobia of snakes, if they see a snake they are likely to have an automatic bodily response; their heart rate would increase, they may start sweating, shaking and their muscles would tense up, amongst other symptoms. This is called the fight-or-flight response. We all experience these symptoms when we are in a situation that causes us anxiety.

If you imagine yourself standing on a stage in front of 10,000 people and being expected to deliver a speech or sing a song – for most people, this would be a terrifying experience which may cause you to freeze and be unable to continue.

A child with SM experiences the fight-or-flight symptoms when they are in a situation where they are expected to speak. If they are in the supermarket and a stranger asks: "What is your name?", their automatic fear response sets in; their heart rate increases, they may start sweating and their muscles tense up. Importantly, their throat muscles tense up to the extent that the words cannot come out. Children often report that their throat feels blocked. This is an automatic response that they have no control over. They physically cannot talk when this happens. They are <u>NOT</u> choosing not to talk - they want to talk but they can't.

The difference between a person who has a fear of snakes and a person with SM, is that the person with a fear of snakes would probably avoid going to places where there are snakes; for example, they would avoid the reptile section at the zoo. They would avoid the situation that causes them anxiety. However, a child with SM cannot avoid being in situations where there is an expectation for them to speak; they have to go to school and they have to engage with the outside world. As a result, they are likely to be in a constant state of being on alert, with fear and anxiety. Imagine a person with an extreme phobia of snakes, being forced to walk through a jungle filled with snakes – a terrifying and extremely stressful situation.

Myths: What Selective Mutism Is Not

The following are myths and are **<u>NOT</u>** true:

1. Children with SM are just shy

Parents of children with SM tell me all the time that their child is not shy. At home when they are comfortable, the child is often the loudest and most extrovert child in the house! Their behaviour is very much influenced by their external environment: where they are and who is present. When their anxiety levels are heightened they become a different child; their body language changes and they suddenly become inhibited. If these environmental factors did not cause them anxiety, then they wouldn't show this change in behaviour. We therefore need to work towards helping the child to overcome their fear of these environmental factors. Children with SM are not necessarily shy; they have an anxiety disorder which is highly treatable.

2. Children with SM are choosing not to talk

As mentioned, children with SM want to talk but when faced with an expectation to talk, their fight-or-flight response becomes activated. As a result, their throat muscles tense up and they cannot talk. This is not a choice. The child wants to be able to join in, have fun and talk to their teacher and friends. Children with SM want to talk but they can't. They therefore need the adults around them to be empathetic, compassionate and supportive.

3. Children with SM are controlling and stubborn

Children with SM are experiencing severe anxiety. If a person has a phobia of snakes and doesn't put a snake around their neck, this is not because they are being controlling or stubborn. They don't put the snake around their neck because it would cause an extreme fear response in them. The child who has never spoken at school is not controlling this – they are not consciously making a decision not to speak; the fear of speaking is paralysing them to the extent that they cannot speak.

4. The child will grow out of it

Parents are sometimes told by professionals to wait for their child to 'outgrow' SM. Please do not listen to this advice – instead, an intervention should be implemented as soon as possible.

The longer we wait, without implementing an intervention, the harder it is for the child to begin talking by themselves. This is because the behaviour becomes more and more entrenched, making it harder for the child to talk the longer we wait. Early intervention is key to helping a child to overcome SM as quickly as possible. It is imperative that the parents and the school begin a structured therapeutic programme so that the child can start to make steps forward.

I highly recommend that schools receive training on treating SM, if they haven't already. Training may be by attending a course on SM, or by reading a book on treating SM.

5. The child must have had a traumatic experience

There may be cases of traumatic mutism, whereby a child is talking and then they suddenly stop due to experiencing a traumatic event, but this is not the same as selective mutism. Children with SM are often from loving homes with parents who are very concerned about the child's SM. What causes SM will be covered shortly.

How Can We Be Sure That The Child Has Selective Mutism?

Parents and schools may be unsure whether the child has SM or is 'shy'. The diagnostic criteria for SM is as follows:

- The child is able to speak freely when they feel comfortable, e.g. at home
- The child doesn't talk in specific situations, e.g. at school or other public situations
- They are able to speak the language fluently
- They have been unable to speak in these situations for more than one month (not including the first month in a new setting e.g. school)
- Their inability to speak is not better explained by a different disorder.

The usual route for a diagnosis in the UK is from a speech and language therapist (SLT). Schools usually have an allocated SLT. Parents should arrange a meeting with the school's special educational needs co-ordinator (SENCo) to discuss referral to the SLT for an assessment.

The usual route for a diagnosis in the USA is by a licensed clinician, most commonly a psychologist, clinical social worker or a speech and language pathologist.

The benefit of gaining a diagnosis is that it gives the child's behaviour a formal label which often leads to the school implementing a formal therapeutic intervention.

However, a diagnosis is not needed to start to make a change. The school and the parent can put interventions in place (with or without a diagnosis) to help the child.

Additionally, even if the child does not fulfil the diagnostic criteria for SM, strategies for SM may still help shy, quiet or 'reluctant talkers' to gain confidence to increase their talking behaviour.

What Causes Selective Mutism?

Children with SM are born with a predisposition to anxiety. Parents often tell me that before their child could talk, they were an anxious baby; they had separation anxiety or were very clingy. Children with SM are also often born with characteristics like sensitivity and perfectionism.

These innate characteristics may or may not lead to SM. They lead to SM if there is a trigger in their environment, such as migration, or starting school or nursery.

Being dropped off at nursery for the first time can be a very traumatic event for any child, especially so for a child who has a predisposition to anxiety. The child is being separated from the person they have spent their whole life with, so this in itself can cause the SM to develop.

I am not suggesting that the child who is very sensitive, or has a predisposition for anxiety should never go to nursery. However, they will cope a lot better with this very big event in their life, if the process is very gradual. For example, if their parent spends time with them in nursery initially and then gradually fades out. This will help the child to adjust and become comfortable in the new environment before the parent leaves.

I have mentioned that children with SM can be very sensitive, so if somebody laughs at them or makes fun of them, this may cause the child to become unable to speak in front of or to this person.

Once the SM has been triggered, maintaining factors keep the SM going. An example of a maintaining factor, could be children in the class labelling the child as not talking: "Laura doesn't talk". If we are given a label it's very hard to break out of this, especially so for a child who is experiencing anxiety.

Other maintaining factors could be adults drawing attention to the lack of speech: "Laura, are you going to talk to me today?", "She never talks to me!" – these comments do not help and make it harder for the child to start talking.

If adults try to force or bribe the child to speak ("If you talk to your teacher, then we will go to Disney Land"), this will heighten the child's anxiety, adding pressure and therefore making it harder for the child to begin to talk.

Another common maintaining factor is parents 'rescuing' the child or automatically talking on their behalf. This is when the child is asked a question and the parent jumps in and answers; this is an intuitive parental response, however, it can be counter-productive and actually reinforces the SM, as it confirms to the child that they are unable to answer themselves.

If there isn't an intervention programme in place at home and school, this can also keep the SM going as the child isn't being guided forward (we cannot rely on the child making steps forward themselves without our guidance).

The above maintaining factors maintain the SM; they keep the SM going.

Our aim should be to firstly remove all pressure regarding speech and to focus on the child having fun. Paradoxically, once this pressure has been removed, once the child feels at ease, they are in a far stronger position to begin to make steps towards speaking.

A small steps programme should then be put in place to help the child to make steps forward with talking (treating SM will be covered shortly).

I would like to emphasise here that parents are never to blame for their child developing SM; if you notice that you have been unintentionally maintaining the child's SM, this is not your fault. There would be absolutely no way of you knowing what to do before learning about SM, so there is no reason to feel responsible.

The Do's And Don'ts When Interacting With A Child With Selective Mutism

Children with SM should be treated in a very specific way in order for their anxiety to be lowered. I have created the following do's and don'ts as a format to follow to help the child to feel at ease. This is the starting point of any treatment programme. These should be followed by people the child doesn't talk to, e.g. family members or school staff.

1. Do not tell the child to speak to you or draw attention to their lack of speech

Never say to a child with SM: "Are you going to talk to me today?"

Children with SM want to talk but as discussed, they cannot. Their level of anxiety is so high that their words just cannot come out. Drawing attention to their lack of speech only increases their anxiety, making it harder for them to speak. Our aim is therefore to help the child to feel as relaxed as possible and remove ALL pressure to speak. Paradoxically, this puts the child in a stronger position to verbalise.

2. Do not give the child over the top attention

Children with SM are often very self-conscious and do not like being the centre of attention. Treat the child exactly the same as you treat other children. It is tempting to give the child extra attention because they do not speak, but this is often counter-productive as being the centre of attention adds to the child's anxiety level.

3. Do not tell the child off for not talking or act frustrated by their lack of speech

The child does not deserve to be told off; they are not being defiant or stubborn, they want to talk but they cannot.

4. Do not ask the child direct questions

School staff sometimes ask the child questions, hoping that finally the child will answer. If the child has never spoken to you, they will not answer your question. This rule applies unless you are asking as part of a planned graded exposure programme (see: 'treating selective mutism', page 25).

Asking a question draws attention to their lack of speech, which only increases their anxiety, making it harder for them to speak. When interacting with the child, it is effective to take part in a running commentary without any requirement for the child to speak. Essentially the adult is describing what they and the child are doing, which removes the pressure for the child to speak. An example of a running commentary could be: "This teddy you have is so sweet, I like the stars on his top... and he is so soft! I used to have teddies when I was a child, but my ones didn't have stars on them like yours! Let's look at the other toys you have..."

An example of a teacher following this technique while interacting with a child in the normal class environment is as follows: "I can see that you've tried really hard with your spellings this week, let's have a look together, so you've spelt 'holiday' right, you've spelt 'elephant' right, hmm... you've made a mistake with 'dinosaur' – it's spelt with a 'u', not a 'w', let me write it down here for you..."

Of course, this would be during routine interactions with the children – the teacher would have similar interactions with other children, but they would have worded their interaction specifically so that the child with SM does not need to speak.

It is important to add here that this technique is used in the beginning stages of treatment; once there is an intervention programme in place, the teacher would begin to encourage speech at school in small steps – more on this in my book for teachers and school staff.

5. Avoid direct eye contact with the child

Direct eye contact increases the child's anxiety levels and implies an expectation of a response and thus can make the situation a lot scarier for the child. Of course, looking at the child is fine, however, avoid staring directly into their eyes for prolonged periods.

6. If the child talks to you, don't act surprised or instantly praise them

When the child speaks for the first time, this is often a very exciting moment, however it is important not to convey this to the child but to act completely normal when they speak. This way they will see that talking evokes a normal response and is not as scary as they may have been anticipating. Therefore, if the child speaks, do not draw attention to the fact that they have spoken, but instead respond to what they have said in a calm and friendly manner.

In order to spread the knowledge of how to interact with a child with SM, I have provided several free resources that can be accessed here:

www.confidentchildren.co.uk/videos

Through this link you can find a useful video called:

'The do's and don'ts when interacting with a child with selective mutism' – this video should be shown to all school staff.

A free summary sheet of the do's and don'ts can also be found via the above link. This summary sheet can be distributed amongst all school staff so that everybody has the basic knowledge needed to be supportive of a child with SM. The do's and don'ts are aimed at individuals who are interacting with the child and not necessarily delivering the therapeutic programme.

I have also put together a free child-friendly video that can be shown to the child's class to help peers understand what the child is experiencing and to explain the key do's and don'ts in a child-friendly way.

Treating Selective Mutism

Following the do's and don'ts creates a supportive environment for the child, removing the pressure to speak. This is the first step to treating SM. The next step is to implement a small steps programme which gradually exposes the child to talking in small manageable steps.

SM in children is treated using behavioural therapy, specifically graded exposure therapy. This is where the child is guided in facing their fear of talking in small manageable steps.

The main therapeutic methods are: stimulus fading (referred to as 'the sliding in technique' in *The Selective Mutism Resource Manual* by Maggie Johnson & Alison Wintgens) and shaping. It is important that the child's anxiety levels are kept to a minimum throughout and that the strategies are embedded within game.

1. Stimulus fading is a technique used to 'fade in' a new person or place. If the goal is for the child to talk to their aunt for example, the child would begin playing a game with someone they are able to talk with freely (e.g. the parent) in a place where they are comfortable (e.g. their living room at home). The aunt would begin by sitting in the background, avoiding eye contact and then very gradually edging closer to the child. The idea is that the child becomes 'desensitised' to the aunt's

presence and begins to tolerate their presence more and more. The aim is that the new person joins in the game and eventually begins to communicate with the child. It is crucial that when fading in, the new person moves at the child's pace and only moves closer when the child is comfortable at the current stage.

2. Shaping is another technique which can be used if there is no conversational partner (e.g. parent) available to do stimulus fading. Shaping involves firstly encouraging the child to make sounds and then building on these sounds so that they are eventually saying words.

I always start with stimulus fading wherever possible as it is the easiest and quickest way to establish speech. This is because the child begins talking to somebody they are comfortable with and therefore we begin with the child talking (even if this means the new person is not in the room), whereas with shaping we start without speech.

Once the parent has faded in a new person, the parent can then begin to fade out by gradually becoming less involved and allowing the child and the new person to play and communicate.

The aim of graded exposure therapy is to gradually increase the number of people the child can talk to and the number of places they can talk in. This is why the techniques must be applied in the real world, so that the child can practice talking at school, in the park, in the supermarket and so on.

As a therapist, I often go out to these locations with the parent and child so they can practice talking in the real world.

Treating SM is complex and can feel quite confusing; I am therefore putting together a comprehensive course for parents where I will talk through this topic step by step. The course may actually be available when you are reading this!

Final Thoughts

Thank you for taking the time to read this book. I hope you now have an understanding of what a child with SM is experiencing. Education, understanding and compassion are the first steps to helping a child with SM.

www.confidentchildren.co.uk offers a variety of free videos so please subscribe to the website and Facebook page to stay up to date with these.

I also offer additional services that you may find beneficial:

- **Skype consultations** with parents / schools where we talk through the specific child's talking behaviour and steps to help the child to overcome SM.

- **School training** where I train the school staff on what SM is and how they can help the child. Crucially, I discuss the specific child's SM and how to help them (as we know every child with SM is different).

- **Direct therapy** with children – one off home sessions where I meet the child and model to the parents how to fade in and how they can fade in other people the child doesn't talk to.

- **Parent training** – parents often unintentionally enable their child's SM – we talk through what parents can start doing to help their child to make steps forward with talking.

- **Intensive therapy** – I spend a week with the child, either at home or at school (or a combination of both) – the aim of the week is to provide a large dose of therapy to jump start the child's progress and to equip the parents and school in continuing the programme.

A list of books that I love and recommend can be found here: www.confidentchildren.co.uk/books. I regularly update this list of books.

I hope that you have gained value from reading this book and ultimately a greater understanding of selective mutism.

Made in United States
Orlando, FL
22 May 2022

18086981R00022